THE
PIANO TREASURY
OF
CLASSICAL MUSIC

OVER 125 GREAT MASTERPIECES FROM THE
BAROQUE, CLASSICAL, ROMANTIC, AND MODERN ERAS.
INCLUDES A COMPACT DISC WITH SELECTED PERFORMANCES.

THE
PIANO TREASURY
OF
CLASSICAL
MUSIC

OVER 125 GREAT MASTERPIECES FROM THE
BAROQUE, CLASSICAL, ROMANTIC, AND MODERN ERAS.
INCLUDES A COMPACT DISC WITH SELECTED PERFORMANCES.

Order No. AM 986348
ISBN-10: 0.8256.3482.2
ISBN-13: 978.0.8256.3482.6

Exclusive Distributors:
Music Sales Corporation
257 Park Avenue South, New York, NY 10010 USA
Music Sales Limited
14-15 Berners Street, London W1T 3LJ England
Music Sales Pty. Limited
120 Rothschild Street, Rosebery, Sydney, NSW 2018, Australia

Printed in the United States of America by
Vicks Lithograph and Printing Corporation

Amsco Publications
A Part of **The Music Sales Group**
New York/London/Paris/Sydney/Copenhagen/Berlin/Tokyo/Madrid

Compact Disc track listing

1. Sarabande from English Suite No.1 (Bach)

2. Allegro from Suite No.7 (Handel)

3. "Pathetique" Second Movement from Piano Sonata in C Minor (Beethoven)

4. Piano Sonata in G (Haydn)

5. Waltz in A-Flat (Brahms)

6. Spring Song (Mendelssohn)

7. Moment Musicale (Schubert)

8. Traumerei (Schumann)

9. Tango (Albéniz)

10. Clair de Lune (Debussy)

11. Humoresque (Dvorák)

12. Gymnopédie No.1 from Trois Gymnopédies (Satie)

13. Album Leaf (Scriabin)

14. Musetta's Waltz from La Bohème

15. Dance of the Sugar Plum Fairy from The Nutcraker (Tchaikovsky)

Piano: David Pearl
Recorded, Mixed and Mastered by Leonard Hospidor

RENAISSANCE AND BAROQUE

CLASSICAL

ROMANTIC

IMPRESSIONIST AND MODERN

LIGHT CLASSICS

THEMES FROM THE OPERA

SCENES FROM THE BALLET

DUETS

Two-Part Invention No. 1

Johann Sebastian Bach
(1685–1750)

Two-Part Invention No. 4

Johann Sebastian Bach
(1685–1750)

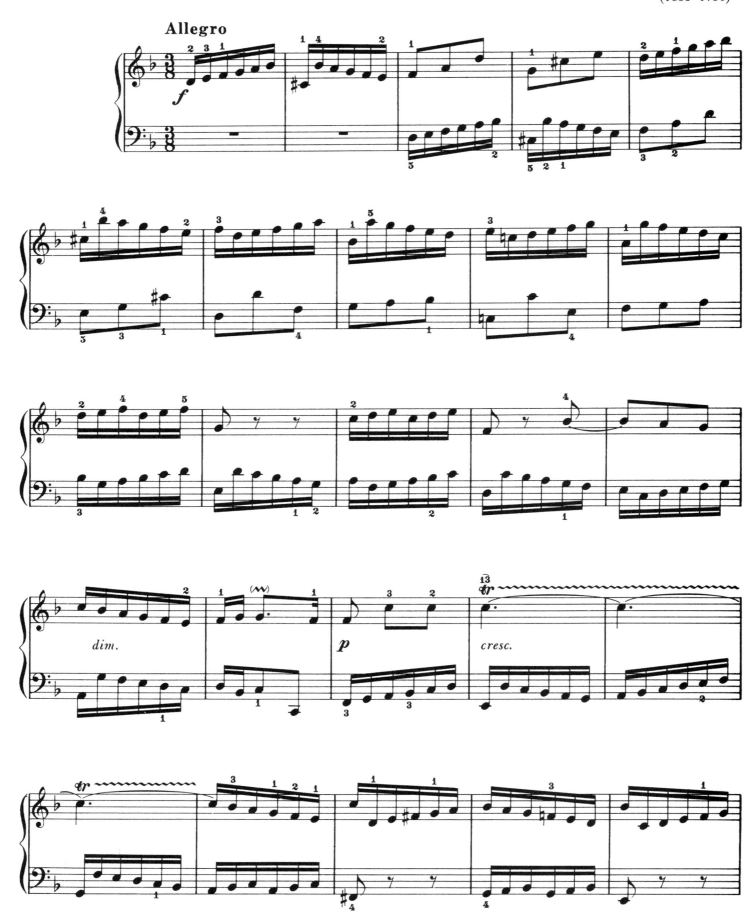

Two-Part Invention No. 8

Johann Sebastian Bach
(1685–1750)

Three-Part Invention No. 9

Johann Sebastian Bach
(1685–1750)

PRELUDE AND FUGUE IN C

from *The Well-Tempered Clavier*, Book 1, No. 1

Johann Sebastian Bach
(1685–1750)

18

CHORALE

Johann Sebastian Bach
(1685–1750)

Sarabande

from *English Suite No. 1*

Johann Sebastian Bach
(1685–1750)

LOURE
from *Third Cello Suite*

Johann Sebastian Bach
(1685–1750)

23

Gavotte
from *Sixth Cello Suite*

Johann Sebastian Bach
(1685–1750)

Allegro moderato

Bourée
from *Second Violin Sonata*

Johann Sebastian Bach
(1685–1750)

Minuet

Luigi Boccherini
(1743-1805)

30

THE PRINCE OF DENMARK'S MARCH

from *Choice Lessons for the Harpsichord or Spinet*

Jeremiah Clarke
(1674-1707)

LES TRICOTEUSES
(The Knitters)

François Couperin
(1668-1733)

Bourée

George Frideric Handel
(1685–1759)

SARABANDE

George Frideric Handel
(1685–1759)

THE HARMONIOUS BLACKSMITH

Air and Variations *Fifth Harpsichord Suite*

George Frideric Handel
(1685–1759)

Var. 4

(2)

Var. 5

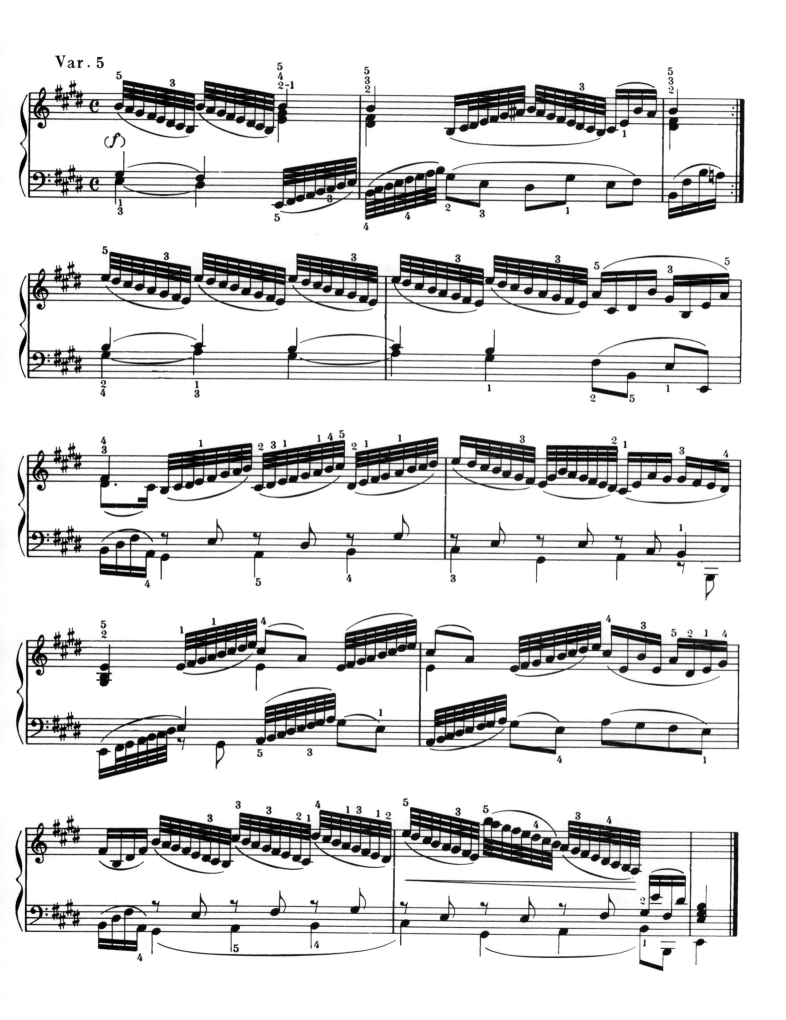

ALLEGRO

from *Suite No. 7*

George Frideric Handel
(1685–1759)

45

HALLELUJAH CHORUS
from *Messiah*

George Frideric Handel
(1685–1759)

Allegretto moderato

TRUMPET VOLUNTARY

Henry Purcell
(1659–1695)

Allegro moderato

SEE THE CONQUERING HERO COMES

from *Judas Maccabeus*

George Frideric Handel
(1685–1759)

Gavotte

Jean-Baptiste Lully
(1632-1687)

Allegro non troppo

Ped. ad lib.

Musette en Rondeau

Jean-Philippe Rameau
(1683–1764)

Tempo di Ballo

Domenico Scarlatti
(1685–1757)

Sonata in D Minor

L. 313

Domenico Scarlatti
(1685–1757)

Allegro ♩= 69

RONDO ESPRESSIVO

Carl Philipp Emanuel Bach
(1714-1788)

Für Elise

Ludwig van Beethoven
(1770–1827)

Poco moto

(Ped. simile)

SONATINA NO. 1

Ludwig van Beethoven
(1770–1827)

Moderato

Romanza
Allegretto

Sonata in G
Op. 49, No. 2

Ludwig van Beethoven
(1770–1827)

Allegro, ma non troppo

Tempo di Menuetto

ADAGIO
from *Moonlight Sonata*, Op. 27, No. 2

Ludwig van Beethoven
(1770–1827)

ALLEGRO
from *Sonata in F Minor*, Op. 2, No. 1

Ludwig van Beethoven
(1770–1827)

84

Minuet in C

Ludwig van Beethoven
(1770–1827)

Trio

Bagatelle in C
Op. 119, No. 2

Ludwig van Beethoven
(1770–1827)

Andante con moto

89

THE GLORY OF GOD IN NATURE

Ludwig van Beethoven
(1770–1827)

Maestoso

PIANO SONATA IN C MINOR

'Pathetique' Second Movement

Ludwig van Beethoven
(1770–1827)

Adagio cantabile

GAVOTTE

François Joseph Gossec
(1734-1829)

Minuet
from *Symphony in D*

Franz Joseph Haydn
(1732–1809)

TRIO

D.C. al Fine

ANDANTE

from *'Surprise' Symphony*, No. 94

Franz Joseph Haydn
(1732–1809)

Maggiore

Piano Sonata in G
Hob. XVI:11

Franz Joseph Haydn
(1732–1809)

Da Capo (al 𝄐)

Menuet

Trio

Menuet da capo

GRAVE E CANTABILE

from *The Seven Last Words*

Franz Joseph Haydn
(1732–1809)

Serenade

Franz Joseph Haydn
(1732–1809)

GIGUE IN G
K.574

Wolfgang Amadeus Mozart
(1756–1791)

Allegro

Minuet in D
K.355

Wolfgang Amadeus Mozart
(1756–1791)

Alla Turca
from *Sonata No. 11*, K. 331

Wolfgang Amadeus Mozart
(1756–1791)

Minuet

from *Divertimento No. 1,* K. 113

Wolfgang Amadeus Mozart
(1756–1791)

120

TRIO

D.C. al Fine

SONATA IN C
K.545

Wolfgang Amadeus Mozart
(1756–1791)

Allegro

Andante

126

Rondo (Allegro)

INTERMEZZO IN A
Op. 118, No. 2

Johannes Brahms
(1833–1897)

WALTZ IN A-FLAT
Op. 39, No. 15

Johannes Brahms
(1833–1897)

PRELUDE IN E MINOR
Op. 28, No. 4

Frédéric Chopin
(1810–1849)

WALTZ IN C-SHARP MINOR
Op. 64, No. 2

Frédéric Chopin
(1810–1849)

Più mosso

Più lento

142

Tempo I

Waltz in A-flat
Op. 69, No. 1

Frédéric Chopin
(1810–1849)

Nocturne in E-flat
Op. 9, No. 2

Frédéric Chopin
(1810–1849)

148

Mazurka in C
Op. 67, No. 3

Frédéric Chopin
(1810–1849)

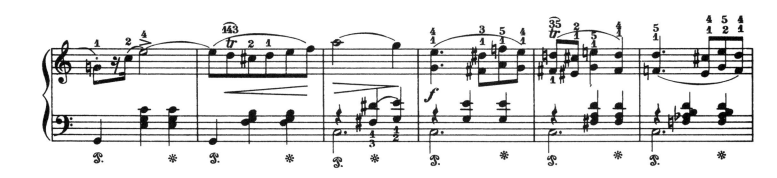

Nocturne No. 5

John Field
(1782–1837)

Cantabile, assai lento

Nocturne
Op. 54, No. 4

Edvard Grieg
(1843–1907)

Tempo I

CONSOLATION
No. 5 from *Six Consolations*

Franz Liszt
(1811–1886)

LIEBESTRAUM
No. 3 from *Three Notturnos*

Franz Liszt
(1811–1886)

Poco allegro, con affetto

162

CONFIDENCE
Op. 19, No. 4

Felix Mendelssohn
(1809–1847)

Spring Song
Op. 62, No. 6

Felix Mendelssohn
(1809–1847)

Allegretto grazioso

170

Capriccio in A

Op. 16, No. 1

Felix Mendelssohn
(1809–1847)

Andante con moto

175

poco ritard. sin' al _ _ _ _ tempo dell' Andante

WEDDING MARCH

from *A Midsummer Night's Dream*

Felix Mendelssohn
(1809–1847)

SPINNING SONG
Op. 67, No. 4

Felix Mendelssohn
(1809–1847)

182

183

Serenade
Op. 90, No. 11

Franz Schubert
(1797–1828)

Moment Musicale
Op. 94, No. 3

Franz Schubert
(1797–1828)

Allegro moderato

(staccato sempre)

Scherzo in B-flat

Franz Schubert
(1797–1828)

Ave Maria

Franz Schubert
(1797–1828)

IMPROMPTU IN A-FLAT
Op. 142, No. 2

Franz Schubert
(1797–1828)

198

Schlummerlied

Robert Schumann
(1810–1856)

REMEMBRANCE
Op. 68, No. 28

Robert Schumann
(1810–1856)

Espressivo

TRÄUMEREI
Op. 15, No. 7

Robert Schumann
(1810–1856)

Moderato

WHY?
Op. 12, No. 3

Robert Schumann
(1810–1856)

205

Sonata
First and Second Movements, Op. 118, No. 1

Robert Schumann
(1810–1856)

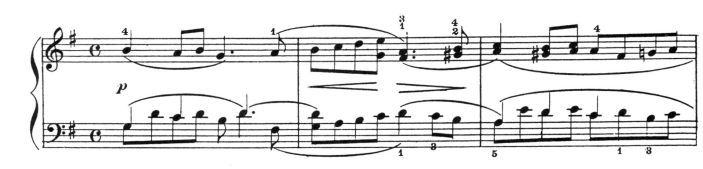

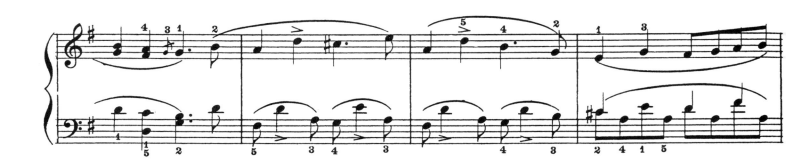

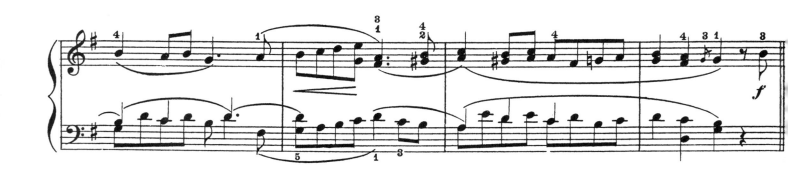

208

210

CHANSON TRISTE
Op. 40, No. 2

Peter Ilyich Tchaikovsky
(1840–1893)

Allegro non troppo
la melodia con molto espressione

WALTZ
Op. 39, No. 8

Peter Ilyich Tchaikovsky
(1840–1893)

Tango

Isaac Albéniz
(1860–1909)

MINSTRELS
from *Preludes,* Book 1

Claude Debussy
(1862–1918)

LA FILLE AUX CHEVEUX DE LIN

'The Girl with the Flaxen Hair' from *Preludes*, Book 1

Claude Debussy
(1862–1918)

CLAIR DE LUNE

'Moonlight' from *Suite Bergamasque*

Claude Debussy
(1862–1918)

morendo jusqu'à la fin

228

HUMORESQUE
Op. 101, No. 7

Antonín Dvořák
(1841–1904)

Poco lento e grazioso (♩=72)

Valses Poeticos No. 2

Enrique Granados
(1867–1916)

TO A WILD ROSE

Op. 51, No. 1

Edward MacDowell
(1860–1908)

With simple tenderness (♩ = 88 M.M.)

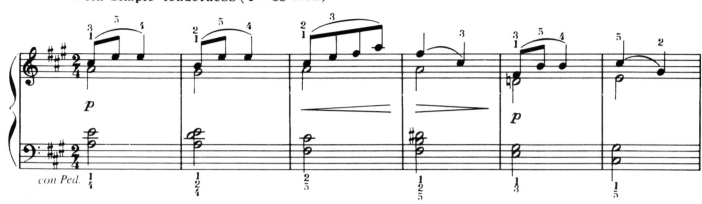

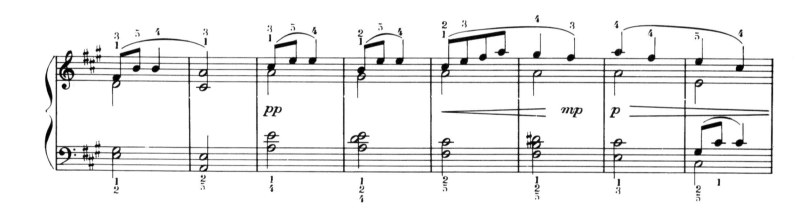

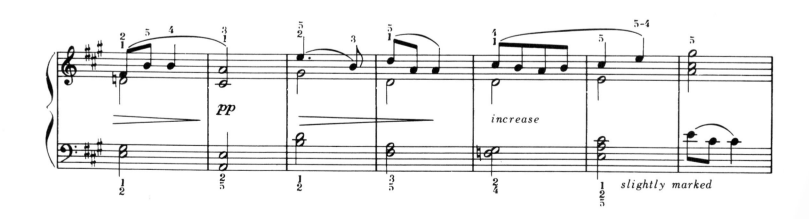

234

ELEGIE
Op. 10

Jules Massenet
(1842–1912)

Lento, ma non troppo

BYDLO

'The Oxcart' from *Pictures at an Exhibition*

Modeste Mussorgsky
(1839–1881)

The Young Prince and the Young Princess

from *Scheherezade*, Op. 35

Nikolai Rimsky-Korsakov
(1844–1908)

Andantino, quasi allegretto

241

Romance
Op. 44

Anton Rubinstein
(1829–1894)

Trois Gymnopédies

Erik Satie
(1866–1925)

1

Lent et douloureux

247

248

2

3

Prelude in A Minor
Op. 11, No. 2

Alexander Scriabin
(1872–1915)

Album Leaf
Op. 45, No. 1

Alexander Scriabin
(1872–1915)

Simple Aveu

François Thomé
(1850-1909)

PRELUDE IN D
Op. 11, No. 5

Alexander Scriabin
(1872–1915)

ENTRY OF THE GLADIATORS

Julius Fučik
(1872–1916)

Tempo di Marcia

La Cinquantaine
(The Golden Wedding)

Gabriel-Marie

Moderato

266

Le Secret

Leonard Gautier

Funeral March of a Marionette

Charles Gounod
(1818–1893)

Danube Waves

Iosif Ivanovici
(c. 1845–1902)

2.

278

Over the Waves

Juventino Rosas

ONE HEART, ONE MIND

Johann Strauss
(1825–1899)

Introduction

Tempo di Mazurka

D.C. ad lib.

Blue Danube Waltz

Johann Strauss
(1825–1899)

289

D. C. ad lib. al 𝄇

Skaters Waltz

Emil Waldteufel
(1837–1915)

La Paloma

Sebastian Yradier
(1809–1865)

CARMEN
(Themes)

Georges Bizet
(1838–1875)

Moderato (Habanera)

Con moto (Toreador Song)

con Ped.

Tempo di Marcia

ben macato

con Ped.

(Toreador's March)
brillante

Ped.   simile

Faust
(Themes)

Charles Gounod
(1818–1893)

Tempo di Marcia (Soldiers' Chorus)

Mouvement de Valse (Waltz)

Allegretto (Flower Song)

Andante (Love Duet)

309

Adagio (Duet "O Moonlight")

310

Moderato maestoso ("Angels Rare, Angels Radiant")

THE MARRIAGE OF FIGARO
(Themes)

Wolfgang Amadeus Mozart
(1756–1791)

Allegro moderato (Sweet Ladies)

314

Tempo di Marcia (Wedding March)

TALES OF HOFFMAN
(Themes)

Jacques Offenbach
(1819–1880)

318

320

La Bohème
(Musetta's Waltz)

Giacomo Puccini
(1858–1924)

WILLIAM TELL
(Themes)

Gioacchino Antonio Rossini
(1792–1868)

Allegretto (Ballet Music)

Allegro (Finale Overture)

Die Fledermaus
(Themes)

Johann Strauss
(1825–1899)

Tempo di Valse (Waltz)

(Ah, what a Feast, what a Night of Joy)

H.M.S. Pinafore
(Themes)

Arthur Sullivan
(1842–1900)

Allegro (We sail the Ocean Blue)

335

Andante (Sorry her Lot)

336

Allegretto (Im called little Buttercup)

338

Allegretto (I am the Captain of the "Pinafore")

Maestoso (For he is an Englishman)

Aïda
(Themes)

Giuseppe Verdi
(1813–1901)

Andantino (Heav'nly Aïda)

342

Allegro moderato (Triumphal March)

LOHENGRIN
(Bridal Chorus)

Richard Wagner
(1813–1883)

VALSE LENTE
from *Coppélia*

Léo Delibes
(1836–1891)

Valse Tempo

Pizzicato

from *Sylvia*

Léo Delibes
(1836–1891)

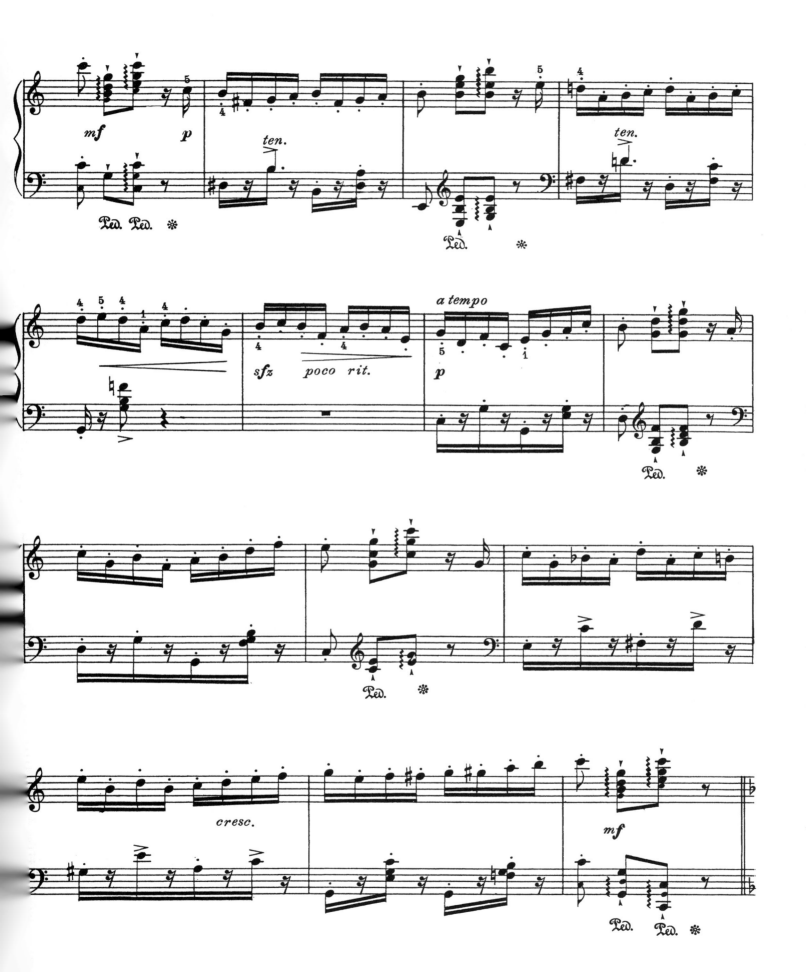

ARAGONAISE

from *Le Cid*

Jules Massenet
(1842–1912)

358

DANCE OF THE HOURS

from *La Gioconda*

Amilcare Ponchielli
(1834–1886)

ENTR'ACTE

from *Rosamunde*

Franz Schubert
(1797–1828)

Andantino

MINORE

LOVE THEME
from *Romeo and Juliet*

Peter Ilyich Tchaikovsky
(1840–1893)

DANCE OF THE SUGAR PLUM FAIRY

from *The Nutcracker*

Peter Ilyich Tchaikovsky
(1840–1893)

DANCE OF THE REED FLUTES

from *The Nutcracker*

Peter Ilyich Tchaikovsky
(1840–1893)

con espressione

Russian Dance
from *The Nutcracker*

Peter Ilyich Tchaikovsky
(1840–1893)

Molto vivace

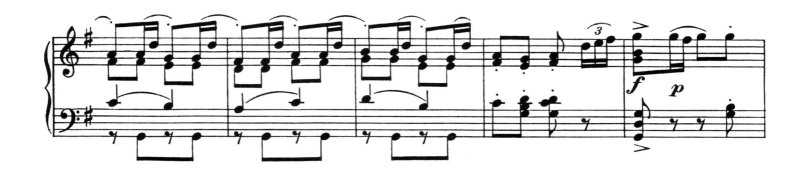

Waltz
from *Sleeping Beauty*

Peter Ilyich Tchaikovsky
(1840–1893)

Tempo di valse

Minuet in G

Ludwig van Beethoven
(1770–1827)

Secondo

Minuet in G

Ludwig van Beethoven
(1770–1827)

Primo

TRIO

D.C.

WALTZ

Johannes Brahms
(1833–1897)

Secondo

WALTZ

Johannes Brahms
(1833–1897)

Primo

PRELUDE

Frédéric Chopin
(1810–1849)

Secondo

PRELUDE

Frédéric Chopin
(1810–1849)

Primo

Polonaise

Antonio Diabelli
(1781–1858)

Secondo

POLONAISE

Antonio Diabelli
(1781–1858)

Primo

CONSOLATION

Felix Mendelssohn
(1809–1847)

Secondo

CONSOLATION

Felix Mendelssohn
(1809–1847)

Primo

Two German Dances

Franz Schubert
(1797–1828)

Secondo

Two German Dances

Franz Schubert
(1797–1828)

Primo

CHANT SANS PAROLES

Peter Ilyich Tchaikovsky
(1840–1893)

Secondo

Allegretto grazioso e cantabile

CHANT SANS PAROLES

Peter Ilyich Tchaikovsky
(1840–1893)

Primo

Allegretto grazioso e cantabile

Secondo

Primo